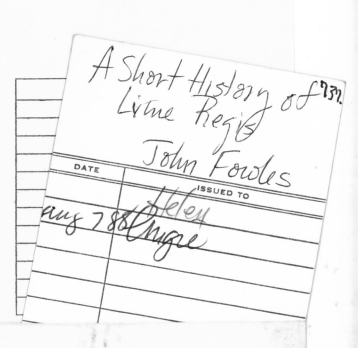

A Short History of
Lyme Regis

the walls of Lyme

Lyme

mylls

A Short History of
Lyme Regis

John Fowles

LITTLE, BROWN AND COMPANY · BOSTON · TORONTO

Designed by Humphrey Stone

Published simultaneously in Canada
by Little, Brown & Company (Canada) Limited

Printed and bound in Great Britain

Foreword

This little account in no way pretends to vie with the far greater and more scholarly work of Hutchins, Roberts and Wanklyn concerning Lyme, though it does try to present the town rather more as a changing and often precarious community than as a stage for a cavalcade of well-known names and events. A major fresh history must now wait on someone with the time and the patience to read and analyze the huge corpus of raw material in the Borough and Colway Manor archives. New documents and discoveries continue to appear; and again and again, in my years as honorary curator of the Lyme Regis Museum, I have had (happily) to revise my own image and views of the town's past.

Of our previous historians, the one I have gained most admiration for is George Roberts (1804 – 1860). He is in my view incomparably our finest, and Lyme will be very lucky if it ever sees his superior. Some material here comes from his copious manuscript notebooks, recently given to the Museum by that doyen of Dorset historians, Mr Harry Johnstone of Poole.

I must finally thank David Burnett of the Dovecote Press for encouraging me to treat at greater length what began as a very humble and unillustrated pamphlet; and now, in his hands, can wear finer clothes.

JOHN FOWLES, 1982

One

Lyme is first mentioned in 774, in connection with a manor and salt rights granted by the West Saxon King Cynwulf to Sherborne Abbey, though no doubt humble salt-boilers and fishermen had lived here for many centuries before that. Stone Age remains have been found close by, and there was an important Romano-British villa-farm at Holcombe, only two miles away. In the Domesday Book Lyme was divided into three manors, and there were at least 27 salt-workers. There is also mention of a mill, no doubt the first on the site of the still existent, though disused, Town Mill. A church existed at least as early as 1145, and very probably the small nucleus of a town formed below it, in what are now Church and Bridge Streets.

Lyme's first great moment came in 1284, when Edward I gave it a royal charter (thus Lyme Regis, or King's Lyme). This was in no way a special honour, but a matter of policy. Edward wanted to make England a conscious nation, centred on the crown. One way he chose to do that was to increase both national prosperity and royal income from it. He was therefore free with such charters (he granted seven others in the same year as Lyme's). Though still kept firmly under the local eye of central administration, in the person of the King's Bailiff or Reeve, these new royal boroughs were allowed considerable trading privileges, a degree of self-government and their own minor courts. They could also send two members to Parliament − a right Lyme enjoyed (or abused) from 1295 until 1832. In return they had to pay an annual rent and other taxes to the royal exchequer.

Lyme was 'let' to the burgesses at 32 marks, the then very large sum of £21.6.8; but the town seems to have been in arrears from the very first year of its chartered existence, and continued to be often so during the next two centuries. In 1299 Edward gave his revenues from Lyme (as-sessed over-all at £35.10.0) as part of his dowry to his new young wife, Queen Margaret. Later kings often had to reduce this fee-farm; or leased it, with its troublesome collection, to others. Richard II granted it for ten years to a man called Merston in 1389; in 1391 Merston was both the rent-collector and the mayor of Lyme, which must have considerably simplified matters. In 1450 Sir Thomas Brooke had the farm at £5 a year; by 1481 it was down to five marks, or £3.6.8., and stayed at this sum well into the 17th century.

Edward's charter was effectively issued in two parts. The first, of 3 April 1284, is a very cursory document. To save themselves un-necessary work, the royal chancellery clerks often used to refer the granted privileges to older models, and with Lyme they chose London and Melcombe Regis (now part of modern Weymouth, and chartered in 1280). This has given rise to a long-lasting local myth that Lyme has the third oldest royal charter. But all the clerks were really doing was citing a famous central and the nearest local precedent, and in fact countless other such charters predate that of Lyme.

Perhaps this first charter was considered too vague. At any rate a much more detailed one was issued a few months later, on 1 January 1285, with very exact instructions as to what Edward would and would not allow. Far and away the most grateful clause for Lyme must have been the freedom from

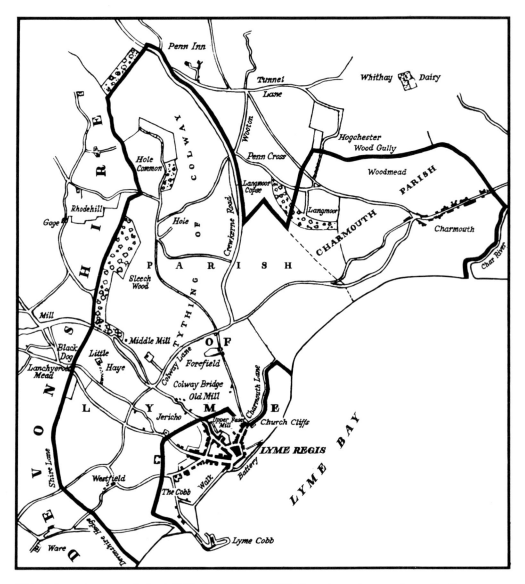

This Reform Act map of about 1832 shows the small area of the royal borough (electing two MPs) in relation to the rest of the parish. The reformed constituency (one MP) was extended to include the parish and also Charmouth. Until 1759 the only carriage road was the Roman one from Charmouth to Axminster via Penn Cross, avoiding Lyme. A Roman branch-track from Charmouth followed the line of Colway Lane towards Axmouth.

toll and lastage — customs and duties in other ports and markets in England and then English France. As with all royal charters the 1284 document was to be many times confirmed and redefined in the centuries to come, as by Elizabeth I in 1591; and again by James I and Charles I. These last three charters especially are full of precious details about the practice and nature of Borough government in their time.

Some of Edward's charters did attempt to found literally new towns, but we know Lyme was trading ('wool out, wine in') with France well before 1284. There had been a market here since at least 1250, and to the anger of the men of Bridport, who felt it was taking business from them. The seamen of Dartmouth also viewed this Dorset upstart with little love. The rivalry had become so serious by 1265 that Henry III himself had to intervene. Finally, the 1284 charter does grant one unusual right — to have a merchant guild. It is unlikely to have been included if there was not already a substantial trading community to take advantage of it.

Edward was therefore clearly encouraging an already established little port. Perhaps he did have some personal affection for it, since he visited Lyme at least once, in 1297. But that is more likely to have been a tour of inspection — and perhaps also to view a galley of 120 oars that he had commanded to be built at Lyme four years earlier.

Though proper historical evidence is lacking we believe early Lyme also gained from a neighbour's misfortune. Lyme Bay has always been a sailor's nightmare, a potential death-trap because of its lack of safe harbours in bad weather — 'verie daungerous in tyme of wynter and tempestes' in

The 13th century common seal of Lyme. The ship is a cog, the merchant vessel of the period, and it flies the arms of Edward I and his first wife, Eleanor of Castile, dating the seal to before 1290.

one Elizabethan description. There was only one sanctuary between the River Exe and Melcombe Regis on the far side of Portland Bill — and that was the River Axe six miles to the west of Lyme. But the mouth of the Axe seems to have suffered some natural disaster, perhaps a cliff-fall, perhaps a shingle-bar blockage, in the 13th century. The ancient parish boundary between Seaton and Axmouth suggests that the river once entered the sea 400 yards west of where it does now, and Lyme may owe a great deal of its rather sudden rise from about 1240 onwards to the ruin of the Axe Haven. (Elizabeth I tried to resurrect the Haven in 1575, but that and later projects came to nothing.)

Two

Despite its royal blessing in 1284, Lyme soon suffered from the perennial nightmare of its history – its very peculiar geological situation. The town is built on, and surrounded by, some of the most unstable land in Britain; and perhaps even worse, it is exposed to the full fury of the sea. The first thing any stranger to Lyme must realize is that the Cobb is not only a harbour; it is just as importantly a gigantic breakwater protecting the town from the great storms out of the south-west. This was fully realized by Sir Francis Walsingham, when he came to Lyme in 1586 to report on it (the previous winter, the Cobb had suffered severe damage) for Elizabeth. He says the Cobb and 'an exceeding number of great piles' protect 'from the violence and fretting of the sea, which otherwise would in short time eat out both the town and land thereunto adjoining'.

Walsingham interestingly explains why the Cobb had not been repaired. All the skilled local workmen had been sent to Dover to make a pier there (a few years later they were at Hastings, for the same reason). The Lyme sea-masons had then, and for at least a century to come, a national reputation, and this was because the rashly sited Cobb was regarded as one of the architectural wonders of England.

Walsingham would have seen a very different structure from the one we see today, since for centuries the Cobb consisted of huge rounded boulders, called cowstones, stacked loose inside massive wooden walls of oak-trunks. No mortar was used. Part of the masons' skill was in fetching the cow-stones from a beach below Dowlands, three and a half miles west of Lyme. They used to float them back between barrels, and this is why repair to the 'Town Barrels' features so frequently in ancient Borough accounts (it does not refer, as was once suggested, to the prevalence of ale-swilling among Elizabethan town councillors). Some forty years before Walsingham, in 1545, the oak-walls themselves had had to be renewed, and the relevant accounts reveal that 61 trunks had to be brought from up to eight miles away (suitable trees nearer Lyme had evidently been exhausted). It was their then rare knowledge of how to transport and 'set' such huge stones and timbers in marine conditions that gained the Lyme men their fame. This construction method did not end until the 18th century, and the Cobb was not fully clad with the present Portland Stone until Regency times.

However, one may speculate as to whether the Cobb really was quite so rashly and perversely sited in its beginning. The old name for where the county boundary with Devon meets the shore some 600 yards west of the Cobb is Devonshire Head, and though there is no headland to be seen today, it is quite possible that the earliest Cobb (first mentioned in 1294, but a date before 1250 is likely) was built in the at least partial lee of a cape long lost to the sea.

The second thing the stranger to Lyme must grasp is that because of the land instability both east and west, Lyme has never been able to expand along the coast. It is forever cramped in its combe between the eroding cliffs, and so can grow only 'backwards' or inland. For many centuries it could not even do that, since most of the parish was in the hands of the owners of Colway Manor (from 1601, the Henley

Monmouth Beach and the Cobb, about 1895. The building in the left foreground is the kiln of a brickyard. The ancient 'island' Cobb began at about where the steps mount to the High Wall. There would have been far less shingle on the beach when Monmouth landed in 1685.

family), who would not part with their estate. (Another effect of this in late Tudor and Stuart times was to drive rich families with money to invest in land out of Lyme entirely.) Of the 1600 acres or so of the parish, the royal borough occupied only the 40 acres of the old town. It had no jurisdiction outside.

One result of all this is strange. In strict numerical terms the population of Lyme has grown surprisingly little since medieval times. It is today about 3,330 – scarcely more than a large village. But in times far past, when the overall national population was much smaller, Lyme was in the same class as now considerable towns like Weymouth, Poole and Dartmouth.

One good check on ancient comparative status survives in lay subsidy rolls (tax assessments) and royal shipping demands. In 1332 Lyme was assessed only just behind Melcombe Regis, the then leading port of Dorset, and it could also boast among its citizens one Richard Kyngman, the second wealthiest man in the whole county. For the Siege of Calais in 1347, Lyme provided four ships and 62 mariners (against five and 96 men from Portsmouth). Lyme and Portsmouth contributed rather little by general standards, but Lyme at least had an excuse. About 1341 another tax roll records that 'the greater part of the town and houses of Lyme have been destroyed by storm and the sea' – and the fact that it could contribute anything at all is remarkable. The present-day Cobb may seem a very minor affair; but for centuries it was a major Channel port.

One strong reason for this was that if the town's geological position was unfortunate, its geographical one – in terms of inland customers — was the very reverse. It provided an export point for a huge hinterland, and stretching well beyond Dorset into Somerset and Devon, as far away as towns like Exeter, Tiverton and Taunton. This was especially so before the 18th century, when the inland road system of England was virtually non-existent and the country's universal thoroughfare was the sea. Even the great merchants of Bristol sometimes preferred to ship through the Dorset ports, rather than risk the corsair-ridden Bristol Channel. Our earliest name-lists suggest that Lyme was attracting tradesmen of all kinds and from far afield. William of Toulouse was one of the very first two Members of

Parliament for Lyme, in 1295. Another man came from Ireland, another from Chelmsford. Taverner, Brewer, Cogger (merchant-ship master), Goldsmith, Peleter (leather-currier), Tanner, Cook, Baker appear among trade-become-proper names.

The Cobb was often 'down' in its early years. No details survive of what happened in 1340, but we have a great many of the results of a savage tempest on November 11, 1377. The Cobb was destroyed and the havoc was appalling. Nearly 80 houses were totally destroyed, over 50 ships and boats lost, many merchants turned paupers overnight. Only some thirty families remained, and most of those were poor tenants. We know about this because the mayor and burgesses told Richard I they could not pay his annual rent, and he appointed a commission of inquiry, whose report has survived. It was very far from the only time this terrible ordeal by sea (to say nothing of other ordeals by the plague and by French raiders, who on at least one occasion set fire

The Great Storm of 22 November 1824. This was the worst storm in the town's modern history; a 23-foot tide coincided with a hurricane wind. The Cobb was breached, yet two old people survived in the houses of the quay. The ship was the Unity, *and eventually went ashore under Black Ven. The crew up in the rigging were saved.*

An engraving from Stukeley's Itinerarium Curiosum. *It is dated 21 August 1723, and shows how the Cobb was then detached from land at high tide. An attempt to bridge Cobb to shore was made about 1700, but it was not finally achieved until 1756. The town remains crowded in the Combe, or valley of the Lim. The promontory marked B is Portland Bill.*

to the town) took place in the 14th and 15th centuries. Again and again the Borough had to go cap-in-hand to the king to ask for special grants and leniency over unpaid moneys.

We may plausibly guess that the medieval town reached some way further into the sea. George Roberts recorded old people's tales in the early 19th century that told of fields and houses standing where now only crabs and oyster-catchers are happy. It is very likely that these are more than mere folk-legends. Roberts himself saw thirty yards of cliff-meadow near the church disappear in thirty years of his own lifetime, a rate confirmed by much more recent estimates. An old enigma of Lyme history concerns a mysterious extension eastward of the royal borough boundary, over land not lived on for centuries. The name of a former head-land there, the Nase or Nash, survives in ancient documents, while the notion that Broad Ledge, now only visible at low tide, was once crowded with houses remains very much alive in local memory. An even older tradition speaks of a Viking harbour on the east side of Broad Ledge.

The town to be seen today is where this constant marine erosion was halted, at least between the Cobb and Gun Cliff (beside the Guildhall), in the 16th century. But its present walled state is misleading in one way. The old town was not walled until the 1750s, and the Cobb Bay not until a hundred years later still. The ancient sea-defences were based on a quite different system, the amassing of huge shingle-banks. These were gathered in a sturdy criss-cross (Walsingham's 'great piles') of oak-groynes, both at right angles and parallel to the shore. Anyone who knows that shingle-drift in the Channel is from west to east will detect

The Cobb Bay in the 1890s; tents took over from machines soon after this.

a puzzle — how could old Lyme ever collect enough shingle with the Cobb firmly barring the way? The answer is simple: it did not bar it. Until 1756 it was detached from land at high tide, simply in order to let the protective shingle through; and before then massive beaches like that still west of the Cobb would have stood before the town itself. A map of the 1820s records shingle-depths there, and even then, after seventy years of 'starvation', they remained far greater than today. Many an ancient ghost of Lyme must have grimly smiled when in the 1970s the highly scientific modern coastal engineers decided groynes must be placed in the Cobb Bay.

Another fatal result of joining the Cobb to land was to reduce the 'scour' in the harbour, and so make it increasingly shallow. Not that the shingle did not also have its disadvantages. One was that it frequently blocked the Buddle, or mouth of the river Lim. 'Buddle' is an ancient mining word, meaning a narrow trough or passage, and since the river was for long the town's main sewer, the consequences were not pleasant. They stank even in Elizabethan nostrils, and payments for 'clearing the chesil from the Buddle' occur in contemporary town accounts.

Three

In economic terms Lyme enjoyed a long heyday between 1500 and 1700, its noon being reached during the reigns of Elizabeth and James I. A Cobb duty list survives from the very beginning of this period, the year 1490, and gives us a good idea of trade then. 'Alyns', aliens or foreigners, had to pay much higher tariffs as buyers or sellers in the town (8d per tun of wine, for instance, as against the 1d charged 'the king's subjects'). The list mentions the following presumably common goods: wine, iron, tin, lead, wood, woollen cloth, canvas, crestcloth (a kind of linen), seven sorts of fish, madder, salt, tar, pitch, resin, bow-staves, battery (objects of brass and copper), wax, saffron, alum, honey, oil, tallow, candles, Flanders tiles, figs and raisins.

Lyme's contacts with Southern Europe long allowed the Borough to offer its distinguished guests exotic luxuries like sweet Malaga and Canary wine (which bore by far the highest duty in 1490). In 1595 the Mayor gave the Marquis of Winchester 'a fair box of marmelades gilted, a barrel of conserves, oranges and lemons, and potatoes'. The latter would have been sweet potatoes, then thought of as a dessert, not a vegetable. Refined sugar was another very precious Elizabethan gift, and little containers of it often accompanied the bottles of wine. Another (and still) much prized Lyme delicacy was 'shrimpis' – what we call prawns today. All such presents were of course tacitly bribes, or demands for support in high places; and considered an essential mayoral expense.

By 1600 Lyme was carrying on a lucrative and far-flung trade not only to the Mediterranean, but also to Africa, to the West Indies and the Americas. Items like gold dust and 'elephant's teeth' could be added to the 1490 import list. A humbler but popular commerce was in Newfoundland salt cod. An agreement of 1608 concerning a Lyme ship, the *Diamond*, sets out in hard-headed detail what the master must do: leave England as soon as possible after March 10, take on the cod at Newfoundland, then sail with it into any part of 'Espayne or Portingall betwixt the North Cape and Calis (Cadiz)'; take on suitable goods in exchange, then come back to England and discharge – and pay the backer of the voyage (Robert Henley of Colway Manor) within thirty days of arrival. The agreement also includes careful clauses against fraud or failure, with a let-out only if 'pirates or enemies' were the cause.

They often were the cause, in fact. The 'Turks' (really Barbary Coast corsairs, their ships sometimes mastered and crewed by renegade Englishmen) haunted the Channel for long after Elizabeth died, and many a Lyme sailor had to languish in Tunis and Algiers while his ransom was collected at home, from local parish to parish, by his relatives. They would be granted a printed royal letters patent for the purpose, since travel out of one's parish in those days was a privilege of the rich, not the poor.

One such 'pass' of 1622, a unique copy, survives in the Lyme Regis Museum. The Lyme ship *Patience*, 40 tons, captain William Hyett, had been for cod to Newfoundland and was caught with its crew of nine men and two boys on its way to Malaga, just inside the Straits of Gibraltar. (The agreement of 1608 firmly specifies that the *Diamond* shall not risk the Straits, for this

This watercolour, probably of the 1830s, is the only surviving view of the old Shambles bell-tower and market-place in Broad Street, burnt down in 1844, and a tragic architectural loss for the town. The 600-year-old market itself did not long survive this blow.

The head of a unique royal letters patent or 'certificate' of 1622, allowing ransom-money to be collected by Captain William Hyett of Lyme for his crew, prisoners in Algiers.

very reason.) Hyett was seemingly returned to England, in order to raise the money for the rest of his crew in prison in Algiers, and the letter is endorsed and signed on the back by the vicar and churchwardens of Northleigh, near Colyton in Devon, with the sum they raised. The Uplyme churchwardens' accounts of the period are full of out-payments to 'poore women with sertificatts', whose husbands had been captured; and who were on the road and begging on their behalf. One wonders what they would have made of a man who then cleaned the Uplyme churchyard, one 'Blackmore' — in reality a blackamoor, and perhaps a corsair galley-slave who ended his days in that tranquil parish.

But even older and more dreaded enemies of Lyme trade lay just across the Channel, in the famous privateer ports like Granville, St Malo and Morlaix. Some used to lie off Newfoundland, waiting for their prey. The *Amity* of Lyme suffered just such a fate in 1703 at the hands of the great Granville pirate, Beaubriand-Levesque; was boarded, and thereafter served as a French victualling-ship. Their depredations also lasted much longer than that of the North African corsairs. They took 20 ships in just two months in 1780, in the area between Start Point and the Isle of Wight. One was the Weymouth sloop *Union*. She was taken in sight of Lyme by a ship playing the old privateer trick of flying English colours; but whose captain, first mate and a majority of the crew turned out to be also English or Irish. Nonetheless, she carried French letters of marque and the sloop was duly sailed to Cherbourg as prize. This menace did not end until Waterloo.

Of course the English themselves were no mean hands at freebooting. A Cobb ship-list of 1578 suggests that several — such as the *Golden Ryall* (*real*, or piece of eight), the *Menyon* (Mignon) and the *Flower de Luce* (Fleur de Lys) — were really foreign prizes turned to home use. The 1578 list names 19

A water-colour of the Cobb and Cobb Bay, artist unknown. A note says: 'Hard gale. 23 July 1860.'

ships from 8 to 110 tons. Eight years later, and two before the Armada, Walsingham reported 23 ships. This may not seem much to our eyes, but a 1589 list gives only 61 ships for all Dorset, and that sets Lyme's importance in truer perspective.

The Armada itself provided further illustration of its importance, though not of the romantic nature our more imaginative historians have sometimes liked to believe. The town did send ships to the English fleet, but the noble defiance and fiery breath of its worthy Elizabethan burgesses seem to have been directed far less at the Spaniards than inland towards neighbouring towns like Axminster and Taunton, who had failed to find their share of the Armada levy. Not a word of the glorious victory appears in their letters to the Privy Council; but a great many of outrage at being asked to foot too much of the bill. It was not the first, nor the last, time that the town has rather played on its physical and economic problems in order to mulct central finance.

In reality more wealth than it had ever known before, or has known since, poured into the town in this period. The benefici-aries were the rich merchants and sea-captains. The most famous of the latter was Sir George Somers, the discoverer of the Bermudas, who was born in Lyme in 1554.

Somers' career is characteristic of one side of Elizabethan Lyme. Though said to be a lamb on land, he was very different at sea – and at times much nearer a buccaneer than anything else. Of fairly humble family, he had by 1590 gained enough prize money to buy two large estates (like so many others he had to look outside the parish of Lyme, but the manor he lived in, Berne at Whitchurch, did give a distant view of the Cobb). Local honours and a knighthood were showered on him, and he died as admiral of the West Virginia Company fleet – and accidental inspirer of Shakespeare's last play, *The Tempest*. The inventory of Berne Manor made just before he sailed on his last voyage gives us a good idea, with its list of rich plate and carpets, of how luxuriously such sailors could afford to live at home. There is only one precious architectural survivor of this great period in Lyme's history, the Tudor House Hotel in Church Street. The town would once have boasted many similar to it.

Much of Lyme's brawling civic and mercantile life then may seem rich and romantic today, and not without pleasure.

Famous visitors came, and theatrical troupes – no fewer than nineteen, including the Queen's and Lord Leicester's Players, between 1573 and 1595 alone. The whole town joined in a week-long traditional Whitsun festival, the Cobb Ale, whose official purpose was to raise money for the Cobb and whose unofficial one was a general letting-down of hair at the coming of summer. But all this was against a much grimmer turn in the town's spirit. No troupes of players appeared after 1595, and a few years later the Cobb Ale was sternly banned for ever. This turn to more serious things was not new. Already, in the 1550s, Queen Mary had dubbed Lyme a heretical (by her Catholic lights) place.

This split may be exemplified from

A Dunster print of the Square, about 1840, from Bell Cliff. The hotel on the left is the old Three Cups. Beyond it, with the coach outside, is the Old Custom House with its market-arcade beneath, for centuries the central meeting-place of the town. Both were burnt to the ground in the 1844 fire.

another remarkable family of Elizabethan Lyme, the Jourdains. One Jourdain, Silvester, was a sailor-adventurer and ship-mate of Somers – it was he who rushed out the first pamphlet (subtitled *The Isle of Devils*) on the Bermudas, when the crew got back to London in 1610, and which Shakespeare must have read. A brother, John, led an equally adventurous life in India, and died there in 1619. But the story of a cousin, Ignatius, is very different. He was born in Lyme in 1561, but then new-born, as he put it, in 1575. The new birth was into the fiercest kind of puritanism. He later became a mayor of Exeter, and also its MP; and was celebrated for his good works. But he showed very little charity towards weaker human vessels, those who did not live by the strictest tenets of the 'righteous' and by 'the testimony of conscience'. It was he who initiated Jourdain's Bill, making death the penalty for adultery; and to whom we owe the first Sunday Observance Act. The drunkards and swearers of Exeter went in profound terror of him. Yet he was also as

fiercely brave in not hiding his contempt for royal or court policy. He once gave a famous retort to someone who asked if he did not fear the president of the dreaded Star Chamber, the Lord Keeper. 'The Lord is my Keeper', said Jourdain, 'I shall not be afraid.' It was the unbending and blindly certain spirit of such men that made, by the time Ignatius died in 1640, the Civil War inevitable.

Seventeenth-century Lyme saw two famous dramas. Like most sea-ports it had grown even more Puritan after 1600, and almost without exception its inhabitants (and new settlers, increasingly drawn to it by its

This photograph of Broad Street is from one of the earliest 'sets' ever taken in Dorset, probably by James Moly of Charmouth. It can be dated to the very early 1850s, and shows the ancient public water-channel, first built in 1551. The Lion Inn did not become 'Royal' until the future Edward VII stayed there in September, 1856.

zealotry and its outspoken vicar, John Geare) took the anti-royalist side in the growing division between King and Parliament during the 1620s and 1630s. Geare seems to have been a man very much in the mould of Ignatius Jourdain. He too refused to knuckle under to the Star Chamber, to episcopal authority or indeed to anything except his own conscience. Reactionary Canterbury and the court knew very well the political dangers of preaching, and the parish church of Lyme has to this day a fine emblem of what Geare's congregation felt about that. The splendid Jacobean pulpit of 1614 is no pious benefaction, but very much a cocked nose at central authority, and a declaration that faith in Lyme would remain 'by the word'. Geare's successor in 1650, Ames Short, was of the same metal. He refused to conform after the Restoration of 1660, and started the first Independent Meeting in Lyme.

But not all in this hotbed of Puritanism

The Gun Cliff area in 1825. Gun Cliff, where the town cannon were kept from earliest times, is the wall on the left with standing figures. It has since been built higher. The house with a central gable just right of where the wall breaks off is the most likely birth-place of Mary Anning. The square building with arched windows and curved roof-parapets is Davie's Baths, opened in 1805.

were of such quality. The career of another preacher-vicar, Thomas Larcombe, born here in 1602, is a good deal less honourable. He proved much too fanatical for his first congregation (at Northam in North Devon), and went to America in about 1640. He proved too much for the New Englanders as well, and had soon to return home − though not so soon that he did not leave an illegitimate child behind. Tavistock then had to suffer him for twelve years; and found him a great deal too fond of 'sack and bowls'. On one occasion he tried to be a chaplain in Cromwell's New Army, and promptly got himself court-martialled for inciting insubordination. In 1659 he spent three months in Exeter jail. In the last years of his

life he foresook religion, and became an apothecary. Larcombe died in 1669, and it is rather difficult to believe that either Jourdain or Geare would have welcomed him to heaven.

In 1644, in the Civil War, the still considerable economic and strategic importance of Lyme led to its being besieged by Prince Maurice and a Royalist army. They heavily outnumbered the Parliamentary forces in the town and expected an easy victory. But the men − and women − of Lyme and their comparative handful of trained supporters endured everything the Royalists could throw at them, including fire-arrows and red-hot cannonballs aimed at the roofs of the then largely thatched town, and an even more dreadful secret weapon still, a reputedly potent-cursing witch. But she was no doubt foiled by the reputed twenty-five preachers of the faith who had come to the defence of the town. The besieged did have two more practical things on their side: Parliament held the Channel seas and so some supplies and reinforcements were got in. They also had a very gifted garrison strategist – Robert Blake, later to be a distinguished admiral.

After facing a heroic two months of resistance the Royalists had to march away with their tails between their legs, and the whole of Parliamentary England rejoiced. Lyme remains a notoriously independent town, and the Siege of 1644 is the noblest celebration of this spirit. By a miracle a diary kept by one of the besieged (Edward Drake, a distant relative of Sir Francis) has survived, and in its pages we can relive every day of those epic two months. The brave women of Lyme, who, like the American pioneers, stood beside their men and loaded their muskets, received their due in a contemporary poem entitled *Joanereidos*, where they were all compared to Joans of Arc.

The story of *Joanereidos* is strange. It was written by yet another fanatical Puritan preacher, James Strong, who, like Larcombe, was evidently no saint in private life . . . and no poet. It was not published (in 1645, then again in 1674) by him, but by his Royalist enemies, and purely to make fun of him and his cause. They did print his poem at the end, but it is preceded by an endless series of virulent lampoons on the poor man, in every known language, from Portuguese to Dorset dialect. Everything about him is impugned, from his morals to

> His feet have eke so strong a scent
> That this our fragrant brother
> Is often sent for with intent
> To cure the women's mother.

The 'women's mother' was a disease, a kind of obstruction of the womb, and burnt feathers was an old folk-remedy for it. Another passage claims that his breath drops spiders dead at three yards' distance; and that even the lice run from his body. But what really outraged the Royalists was Strong's notion that women could be as brave as men; and an equal venom is shown for the 'viragoes' and 'poor female cattle' of Lyme. The shoe is on the other foot now, and we may read Strong as a sincere, if naïve, early defender of sexual equality. Besides, the fact that the women did behave

with exceptional courage in the Siege is well attested from other sources.

The second 17th century drama was much more a tragic folly. In 1685 the Duke of Monmouth landed just beside the Cobb to launch his doomed attempt on the crown of his uncle, James II. One reason he chose Lyme was the memory of the 1644 Siege, and the certainty that he would find himself in a still fervently anti-papist part of the country; while it was also handy for the real centre of Westcountry unrest, Taunton. He may also have known that in 1684 Lyme had not been allowed, for the first and only time in its history, to elect its own mayor; but had had one imposed on it by the Privy Council – a safe Royalist, Gregory Alford. Alford was one of those who duly alerted London of the landing on June 11th. Monmouth recruited in Lyme for a few days, and then set off on his fatal march northwards.

Lyme paid for it after Sedgemoor, when Judge Jeffreys descended on the West to exact retribution; on September 12th, only three months later, twelve rebels were hung and eleven quartered at the very place of landing. Jeffreys paid a secret visit to Lyme the day before, on his way from Dorchester to Exeter, perhaps to ensure that Gregory Alford could see the executions through without causing a riot. But there was an even more sinister reason. Jeffreys was always open to the bribe; and the youngest of those condemned to die at Lyme, the 19-year-old William Hewling, had both a rich grandfather and a remarkably brave and determined sister, called Hannah. William was hanged, but not quartered. The next day his body was taken to Lyme churchyard, surrounded by the young gentlewomen of the town (he was a strikingly handsome young man), to be buried. Hannah had paid the Lord Chief Justice £1000 for this small grace; and a fortnight later, at Taunton, had to pay the same sum again when William's brother Benjamin was also hanged. (On another occasion she tried to stop Jeffreys' coach by clinging to a wheel, and would not let go until she was whipped away.) The Lyme Regis Museum recently acquired her manuscript memorial of her two brothers' terrible martyrdoms. Their last conversations with her still burn with that intense and primitive fervour of the non-conforming (in their case, the Baptist) tradition in the West of England.

The eleven other victims at Lyme were quartered, and these grisly remains were hung in chains in various parts of the town, such as the Cobb Gate; and were to remain there until the Revolution of three years later. Stukeley claims that some could still be seen in 1723.

But the Bloody Assize was far from the first penalty Lyme had had to pay for being a famous cradle of the dissenting tradition. Soon after the Restoration of 1660 Alford and another of the rare local Royalists, Robert Jones, started a cruel campaign of persecution against the various sects into which the old Puritans had divided. There were by then strong Baptist (their first minister, Sampson Locke, was another of those hanged on Monmouth Beach in 1685), Independent and Quaker meetings in the town. Unable to worship normally, the congregations were driven out into the open air, most famously at White Chapel Rocks in the Undercliff and in Sleech Wood north of Lyme. A place in the Undercliff where Jones is said to have spied on those going to the 'Mount Sion' of Chapel Rocks is still known as Jones's Chair.

There are two famous stories about his death. In one, when he died at the Great House, Broad Street, a sinister hearse drew up outside, driven by an undertaker with cloven hooves. The hearse took the corpse up the street — but there did the impossible and turned down the narrow alley of Sherborne Lane. It was last seen galloping down to the River Lim, turned Styx, amid sulphur, lightning and shrieks of agony. The other story tells of a Lyme ship in a fog near Sicily. Suddenly a strange ship loomed close, with myriads of devils in its rigging. The Lymer gave the old hail: 'Where bound? What cargo?' And back came the answer from the satanic ship's master: 'Out of Lyme, for Mount Etna with Robert Jones.'

Sherborne Lane, about 1900. It is a Saxon thoroughfare, and took its name from the estate given to Sherborne Abbey in AD 774. This lay west of the river and was called Lyme Abbots — as opposed to King's Lyme on the east bank.

'Chapel' was to rival 'church' in Lyme for at least another century. Lyme mothers continued to threaten naughty children with the fearsome bogey of Robert Jones well past 1800; while Monmouth remained a flawless hero in popular memory. A quatrain everyone in old Lyme knew by heart was one he was said to have written soon after landing:

> Lyme, although a little place,
> I think it wondrous pretty;
> If 'tis my fate to wear a crown,
> I'll make of it a city.

Perhaps the finest individual emblem of the dissenting spirit in Lyme was born in Coombe Street about 1668. His name was Thomas Coram. He became a ship's captain,

A James Moly photograph from the top of Broad Street, early 1850s. On the left may be seen the narrow three-storied porch of the Great House, demolished in 1913. On the right the house below the one with the columned doorway was Mary Anning's fossil shop from 1826 on.

then a very successful general merchant, in both Europe and America. In America he had already shown himself one of the first white men to try to remedy the injustices done on the Indians. But he devoted all his last years to just one object: the plight of the then countless illegitimate children of London. In his time these unfortunates and their mothers were thought beneath consideration, let alone concern, and he met both ridicule and indifference. But finally (with the help of men like Hogarth and Handel) he achieved what we now see as one of the most remarkable leaps in social conscience of his entire age: the establishment in 1745 of his famous Foundling Hospital. Dear old Coram died in 1751, a complete pauper. Every penny of his fortune had been 'lost' in the hospital. Lyme has more famous names attached to it, but none of kinder memory.

Four

Lyme was enduring, in the year Coram died, a far deeper trauma than those of the Siege and Monmouth's rebellion. Though its fortunes had first begun to slip about 1650, it remained, even thirty years later, a still important port. A list of 1677 makes Lyme the fourteenth among considerable ports in the whole of England; its Customs receipts for the preceding year were £4643, while Liverpool's were only £3507. Nor did its population fall far below that of now huge cities like Birmingham and Sheffield. But from 1700 its economic decline became abrupt and nearly fatal. Three major factors were the general reduction of the West-country cloth-trade before the better-organized competition from the north of England, the increasing size of merchant ships (for which the Cobb became too shallow), and the inaccessibility of Lyme by land.

Perhaps the strangest fact about the town is that no wheeled traffic could get into it until 1759, when a turnpike was built. The only 'wheel-road' before then was the ancient Roman road (the present A35) between Charmouth and Axminster, which gave Lyme a wide berth. All land transport-ation before 1759 had been done by pack-horse and seam or dorser — respectively wooden boxes and huge baskets slung on each side of a horse's back. It was by dorser that Lyme fish went to London (in what state it arrived one does not like to think); while 'seam' is an almost standard measure of bulk in old accounts, for materials like stone and timber.

By 1750 Lyme was in a state of frightening decay. Many of its great merchant-houses empty or in ruins, most of its ancient cloth-making and import-export trades gone with the wind, its population dwindled to less than a thousand souls. George Roberts gave a famous description of it, culled from the oldest survivors of that rockbottom of apathy and hopelessness. One of the few well-to-do citizens of the time, Robert Fowler Coade, wrote in 1760 that the town was several years in arrears over the Land Tax; and threatened that if they could not get it eased, then he and the other principal inhabitants would 'give up all our houses, then desert the town'. Many houses were already 'fallen, pulled down or unoccupied'. His letter is remarkably similar in tone to the frequent medieval pleas to the King for aid and relief.

Part of the apathy was caused by the town's parlous political state. From the 1730s the parliamentary borough fell into the hands of a Bristol family, the Fanes, whose

The George Inn in Coombe Street, destroyed in the 1844 fire. The George was the great packhorse inn of old Lyme, and was where those who came to join Monmouth gathered. Woodcut after a sketch by George Roberts.

head became the Earl of Westmorland. They gained their foothold through John Scrope and Henry Holt Henley, the MPs for Lyme. Both were related by marriage with the Fanes, who had no human interest whatever in the town, and ran it with a ruthless contempt for its ancient freedoms and privileges. All they wanted were its two seats at Westminster, and they ensured them by restricting the vote to their own friends and placemen — many of whom were never seen in Lyme except on election days. They also totally corrupted the Lyme Customs service. After 1782 Customs officers were supposed by act of parliament to stay aloof from politics; in Lyme they continued to be the local managers — or Mafia — for their Bristol masters. No innkeeper who allowed anti-Fane talk in his rooms could expect any mercy when his licence came up for renewal before the (Fane-appointed) justices of Lyme. Another of their tricks was to allow sea-walls below opponents' houses to fall into disrepair. All attempts to oust them failed, and they held the town until the Reform Act of 1832. Lyme was one of the 55 boroughs then reduced to a single MP; and in 1867, one of the five disfranchized completely.

The general effect the Fanes had on Lyme was summed up in an 18th century verse:

Satan resolved to take a rout
And search the country round about
To find where he could fix his seat,
Where fraud, hypocrisy, deceit
And avarice did mostly dwell
To furnish candidates for Hell.
One of his agents by his side
With a malicious grin replied,
"Give o'er your search, 'tis wasting time —
You'll find all you can wish in Lyme."

The hell-furnishing Fanes did not, however, have it entirely their own way. The Coade family, who were educated and hardworking Baptists with Devon wool-trade connections, bitterly opposed their methods from the start. A long letter from Robert Fowler Coade's brother George to John Scrope in 1747 remains a classic denunciation of pocket borough chicanery and of Scrope himself. The Coades' opposition was not only political. They were able to bring at least some work to the dying town. There remained a trade in Devon serge to Italy, and the Coades insisted on having it finished in Lyme and carried on Lyme ships, even in the face of protests from their own Exeter workers. The town split into two parties, the Townites (or 'Blues') and the Fanites (or 'Yellows'), roughly equivalent to Whigs and Tories.

Voters in parliamentary borough elections consisted traditionally in Lyme of three bodies: the burgesses (the mayor and corporation), the freemen of the town, and the freeholders. The Fanes could 'fix' the first two categories, but not the third; and in the end they were reduced to hiding the town charters and pretending that the freeholders had never been allowed a vote. Their main opponent in the later 18th century was Captain Thomas Follett, an army man, aided by Captain Warren Lisle. Lisle, a Preventive Service officer, had owed his early success to the Fanes, and even served as mayor of Lyme at their behest; but later, sickened by the corruption they thrived on, he turned against them. Follett did his best to penetrate the town archives for evidence of ancient practices and rights, and in pursuit of that became effectively the first historian of Lyme. Among other things it is to him that we owe Drake's diary of the 1644 siege. The original has disappeared since he meticulously copied it in the 1780s.

Handsomely the strangest character of this period was Captain Thomas's father, Benjamin Follett, who somehow managed to be Town Clerk to the Fanite Corporation for nearly sixty years (from 1735 to 1792), while remaining a convinced Townite in his own beliefs . . . whence his nickname of 'Blue Devil'. Quite how he tolerated them for so long, and they him, remains a mystery. His successor, George Smith, was an Axminster lawyer and mere creature of the Fanes. He cut a poor figure at the Municipal Commission Enquiry of 1833, when a century of Fanite maladministration had finally to be accounted for. The

Old Lyme, enlarged from a mid-Victorian miniature drawing, and curiously shown from an aerial viewpoint. The Assembly Rooms stand behind the horse and cart. The building with a chimney behind them is a former cloth factory at Mill Green. Note the oak groyne and depth of shingle.

ignorance he had of the town's constitution was amusingly displayed when he informed the Commissioner that the 1284 Charter had been granted at a mysterious French town called Kaer-en-Arvon. Unfortunately there was no one present to tell him that Caernarvon is in Wales. Again and again he was reduced to explaining abuses by saying they had arisen 'by prescription' – ancient custom.

Alas, the Coades and Folletts and their supporters were exceptions to the rule, and by 1832 Lyme could not think of politics except in terms of vote-selling, and it continued in its old ways. It was the subject of two Parliamentary Enquiries in the 1840s, and *The Times* gave Lyme the not very proud distinction of being the most infamous sewer in British politics. However, one latter-day compensation of the two huge Enquiry reports is the very vivid picture they give of the Early Victorian town. The revelations of the ubiquitous electioneering corruption have their lighter moments. The ingenious way in which one young gentleman managed to extract fat bribes from both Whigs (or Liberals) and Tories, without either side realizing, belongs more to high comedy than anything else. He pleaded a touching uncertainty over his political beliefs; but it emerged that by some strange coincidence they always blew with the same wind as the latest 'present' or 'loan' he had received.

Five

Lyme had long been saved, by the 1840s, from its state of near-death in 1750. Salvation came, strangely enough, from the very thing that had so often brought devastation: the sea. In that same year of 1750 a Dr Richard Russel published an obscure Latin treatise on the virtues of sea-water, both for bathing and drinking. (Early visitors would be seen on the beach, tankard in hand, taking their doses from the source.) His work was soon in English, and immensely popular, perhaps mainly because the sea was declared a cure-all for just the sort of illnesses (from gonorrhea to gout) that the only people who could then afford to go to the sea, the self-indulgent rich, increasingly suffered from. Of course the same people had long frequented inland spas like Bath, and Russel was not the first doctor to extol the sea medicinally. Indeed Scarborough had been a sea spa since the 1730s. It was just that his book was perfectly timed to coincide with the early rise of the Romantic Movement, and the general discovery of the beauties of 'wild' nature.

There was a good enough reason why few people had ever thought of the seaside (at least in Southern England) as a place for health and pleasure before then. It had remained a frequently dangerous place all through the 17th century. Land attacks by the Barbary Coast corsairs and French privateers had been commonplace occurrences all along the Western seaboard. In 1690 Lyme faced the awesome sight of the 110 sail of the French Channel fleet standing off the town – particularly awesome because five days earlier the Frenchmen had landed and sacked our Devon neighbour Teignmouth. Fortunately for Lyme they sailed away after a brief exchange of cannonades. The years since then had been comparatively quiet. In 1740 someone sent to inspect Lyme's defences reported that 'because of the long peace' the town's antiquated cannons and lesser firearms were not even in a usable state.

The conversion from defunct trading-port to fashionable seaside resort took place with remarkable rapidity, in historical terms. The very first mention at Lyme of the new 'sea mania' comes in 1755, in a recently discovered bill for the painting of a 'bathing-house', probably near the Buddle. The town was then lucky in attracting the affection of one of the most humane and enlightened men of the century, the radical philanthropist Thomas Hollis (1720 – 1774). A determined democrat and republican, all his heroes came from the libertarian side of the 17th century, and he spent his life propagating those ideals in both Europe and America. Any movement against political tyranny was sure of his support, both financial and educational (in the form of beautifully bound copies of his favourite books). He was one of the great benefactors of Harvard University, in America; and was to prove as much for Lyme.

He had retired to an estate at Corscombe, near Beaminster, and spent much time here in the last few years of his life. He rented permanent rooms at the old Three Cups Inn at the bottom of Broad Street, and defiantly (he was no friend of the Fane family) dubbed them 'Liberty Hall'. In effect he took still moribund Lyme by its shoulders and gave it a sharp shake, showing that its future lay in what we now call tourism.

To that end Hollis bought much

Part of an 1819 etching and engraving by George Cruikshank, after a sketch by the novelist Captain Marryat. It is entitled Hydromania *('water madness'). Marryat's sister lived at Charmouth at this time. Note the shipyard to the left. Only one copy of this print is known to exist.*

ramshackle property in the town, simply to have it demolished and the prospect improved. He bought land by the shore and in 1771 created the first public promenade – today the eastern end of Marine Parade (a crass municipal name for what many in Lyme still call by its Regency one – the Walk). He set on foot an Assembly Rooms, modelled on the famous ones at Bath. And finally he brought off a great 'publicity coup'. Knowing that his friend the Earl of Chatham – not his friend when he first took his undemocratic title – had a sickly son, he persuaded him to bring the boy to Lyme in 1772 for the sea air. The 'sickly son' was

William Pitt the Younger, destined soon to become an even greater prime minister than his father. William and his elder brother, Lord John Pitt, evidently enjoyed Lyme and its society, and so did their father. He even wanted to buy the house they stayed in, the Great House, but the Coade family, who then owned it, refused to sell. Letters from Hollis and Chatham give us a pleasant picture of this holiday, with the elderly Hollis and the vivacious boy deeply engaged, during excursions, in political and philosophical argument.

Though Hollis died in 1774, his vision was amply fulfilled in the next two or three decades. Lyme became especially popular with those recuperating from the Bath season, which meant that its high season was much later than nowadays, from September to November; and for many years still, people did not bathe for mere pleasure, but for medical reasons. Many of these visitors

29

A photograph from the Cobb Gate Jetty of about 1905. The Assembly Rooms (pulled down in 1928) are on the left. The sea-walls to the far right were not built till the mid-18th century. The photograph also vividly shows how jetties amass shingle to their west, and starve beaches to their east.

were distinguished. The one Lyme is proudest of is Jane Austen, who stayed with her family in 1803 and 1804 (most probably at the still existent Pyne House in Broad Street), and later set part of her novel *Persuasion* here. There survives a long letter to her sister Cassandra, written on 14 September 1804. Though she is gently caustic about the provincial pretentiousness of the town, she evidently enjoyed it and reveals

---

◁ *The Walk, about 1833, before the Cobb Bay was walled. The walls projecting on the beach are part of the West Fort, built in 1627 and demolished in the late 1850s to make way for the Lower Walk, or Cart Road. Beyond the Fort is a still existent jetty, planned and created by the geologist De La Beche in the 1820s.*

that that morning 'the bathing was so delightful and Molly (her maid) so pressing with me to enjoy myself that I believe I stayed in rather long, as since the middle of the day I have felt unreasonably tired'. But she talks also of walking on the Cobb and dancing at an Assembly Rooms Ball; she was twenty-nine years old, and no frail invalid.

Though Jane Austen bathed in the sea from a machine, indoor baths soon became popular. The first was built by Giles Davie in that same year of 1804, where the Marine Theatre now stands; and was to be followed by two more. These baths offered not only private cubicles and warmed water, with attendants, but newspapers, refreshments and even card-tables. A scene in an amusing satirical poem of 1818, *The Lymiad*, describes an impromptu picnic and dance at Davie's Baths. The technological miracle of Lyme that year, however, was an indoor commode in one of the lodging-houses, not very tactfully placed in a cabinet built in the corner of the dining-room.

The Assembly Rooms were the centre for fashionable society, and *The Lymiad* also gives us a vivid picture of life there. Snobbery and backbiting reigned, amid the balls and gambling card-parties, the flirts and tyrannical old ladies, the gruff captains and pretentious young men. The snobbery was to continue well into Victorian times. It is said that the tea tycoon, Sir Henry Peek, built his huge 1870s mansion at Rousdon (at a cost of £240,000, and now Allhallows School) out of mortification at having been refused membership because he was deemed 'in trade'; while a lady still alive recalls being severely reprimanded in the early 1920s for having gone to tea with a local clergyman and his wife − not because they were not eminently respectable in themselves, but because some remote relation was known to own a famous Bond Street jeweller's shop.

Even then one was still 'Army or Navy, or nothing'.

Other early visitors − especially retired or half-pay naval officers − chose to settle, and from the 1790s elegant Georgian and Regency 'villas' and 'cottages' (often rather grand houses in fact) began to appear on all the hillsides surrounding the ancient town. The fine view was much sought after, as many house names of the period show: Summerhill, Bellevue, Belmont, High Cliff, and so on. For a time Lyme was known as 'The Naples of England', with Golden Cap cast as Vesuvius; a title it could more justly claim for its (still) unusually mild winter climate, which near the sea allows the growing of many plants normally too tender for Britain, such as mimosa.

Six

A whole new class of entrepreneurs arose in Lyme to meet the needs of the visitors. A family called England is typical. They ran or owned a hotel (now the Royal Standard Inn at the Cobb), an indoor baths, bathing-machines, a circulating library, a private school and a small passenger vessel. In Hollis's time there was virtually only one inn that catered for well-to-do visitors to Lyme, the old Three Cups; by 1820, half a century later, there were several, and many boarding-houses, besides houses and furnished apartments to rent. Property-owning became good business. The sharp-tongued anonymous authoress of *The Lymiad*, who lived

at Bath, complained (like Jane Austen before her) of the absurdly cramped and 'old-fashioned' conditions many well-bred visitors had to put up with at Lyme; but even she seems to have regarded it as more of a joke than anything else, and amply compensated for by the pleasures of sea and countryside, of sailing-races off the Cobb and picnics in the Undercliff (then a much more open and meadowy place than now).

All this brought about great changes lower down the social scale. Very soon in our apprentice books it is the 'service' trades and crafts like tailoring and shoemaking that far outnumber the old Lyme staples of cloth-making and shipping. The sound of the looms continued until the 1830s in a small factory at Mill Green. Related trades survived a little longer. There was a silk throwstery (making silk thread) in mid-Victorian times; and a few last lacemakers, although the art of the old bone or pillow lace was dead much earlier. This lace had generally been done as outwork for the more famous centres of Honiton and Beer. It was once an important cottage industry for the women of Lyme, who would sit in their whittles at their doorways, gossiping as they worked. The whittle, a kind of blanket-shawl dyed crimson, was once almost a uniform for the working women of the town. Roberts speaks of the river of red that would issue from church and chapel door on Sundays. Alas, it could not survive the arrival of female fashion from outside.

A previously unmentioned trade of Lyme was ship-building, though few records survive before 1766. But between that year and 1852 no fewer than 102 ships, mainly topsail schooners but including a 12-gun Royal

JEFFERD'S

HOT, COLD, AND TEMPERATE

SEA-WATER

BATHS.

Also, Pump, Shower, and Limb Baths.

N. B. The Baths are the largest in Lyme, although at the same Price, and contain more Water, which is regularly pumped every day, pure from the Ocean.

An advertisement from Roberts's Guide, about 1829. Jefferd took over Davie's Baths, on the site of the present Marine Theatre.

34

The Lyme Regis, *one of the last large sailing-ships built at the Cobb. She was launched in 1849, but was lost in South Africa ten years later. The water-colour is by Joel Hallett, a local shoemaker. He obtained his delicate browns by soaking cigar-butts in water.*

Navy brig called HMS *Snap*, were launched. The Cobb yard's last 'keel' was surprisingly large, the *Salacia* of 475 tons.

But in this same period between 1780 and 1830, while most of the town slept at night, another age-old maritime industry thrived. This was smuggling. Lyme was the Revenue Service's headquarters for the notoriously 'bad' coast between Burton Bradstock and Beer. Their cutters (fast little sailing-ships armed with small cannon, nothing like the heavy naval rowboat of more recent times) lay in the Cobb, while riding officers patrolled the cliffs, looking for all sail out of the south and also contacting the informers on whom their knowledge of 'runs' so often depended. The chief picking-up places (even at the height of the Napoleonic

Wars) were Cherbourg and Guernsey, and the usual method was not to bring contra-band tobacco, brandy and silk straight on land, but to sink it offshore in weighted and water-tight barrels, for later collection – when the coast was literally clear. Charton Bay, two miles west of Lyme and still one of its loneliest beaches, was a favourite landing-place, so popular that the Revenue Service had finally to establish a look-out post there.

The most famous local man was John Rattenbury of Beer, who married a Lyme girl in 1800 and often worked out of the town – and sometimes ran through it, chased by the press-gang. He was later nicknamed 'The Rob Roy of the West', and was almost universally admired for his daring and seamanship . . . and altruistic courage. He also worked as a pilot, and several times saved, in those days before a lifeboat service, ships in distress. On one occasion he was summoned to the House of Lords to give technical evidence about the

coast before an inquiry. Their lordships greatly liked his profound practical knowledge and bluff humour. But old leopards do not change their spots. A week or two after this moment of respectable glory Rattenbury was back on the Cherbourg run. His *Memoirs*, ghosted at the end of his life, remain a classic of smuggling literature, and worth five hundred romantic fictions on the theme (including Walter Besant and James Rice's *'Twas in Trafalgar's Bay*, based on Rattenbury and set round Lyme).

Professional smuggling continued until at least 1867, when a Coastguard Confidential Orders Book demands a sharp watch be kept for the ketch *Your Name* of Lyme. The master, Abraham Cox, is called 'a notorious smuggler'. The *Your Name* collected many stories. On one occasion she turned up at Plymouth Docks with only half the cargo of limestone that she was supposed to be carrying. The crew duly weighed out the half load on the quayside; returned in the middle of the night and loaded it all back in the hold; then weighed it all out again the next morning . . . and so satisfied the manifest. Her crew were not always volunteers; a favourite trick was to make innocents very drunk at the old Cobb Arms. When they woke up, they would find themselves far out at sea, and with no choice about their work for the next few days or weeks.

◁ *The Cobb and old town, about 1840. The little one-storey house, extreme left on the shore, was the Marine Circulating Library, now Library Cottage. Just right of it stands England's Baths, built in 1839.*

Seven

One special category of the affluent and educated Georgian new-comers to Lyme must be mentioned. The decades on either side of 1800 saw the birth of a science, that of palaeontology – the study of fossil life. The instability of the ground on which Lyme is built may be something residents could happily do without; but for the scientists it soon made the town a Mecca. (Its fossil potential had been noted as early as 1673, by John Ray.) The grey Jurassic is not only exceptionally fossil-rich, but also always crumbling away to reveal fresh material. Almost all the famous early palaeontologists came to Lyme.

One of them, Henry Thomas De La Beche (pronounced Beach), spent the vital years of his adolescence here, while two others, William Buckland and John Conybeare, had close local connections. De La Beche arrived in Lyme (in 1812) by chance; he was sixteen, and very much in disgrace, as he had just been dismissed from his military college for insubordination. He came to Lyme because his mother had married for the third time (in *The Lymiad* she is rather unkindly nick-named Madame Trois-Maris). Her new husband was William Aveline, who lived at what is now Lloyds Bank in Broad Street. Through his stepfather De La Beche met two chief members of a lively little scientific circle in Lyme, Dr Carpenter (surgeon and coroner of Lyme, and an early collector of fossils) and George Holland, a keen meteorologist and phrenologist. In 1816 they took the twenty-year-old on a geological tour of Northern England and Scotland, and fixed him in his true vocation. He was to become perhaps the greatest practical geologist of his age – and a lifelong

disproof of the contention that outstanding scientists are always humourless mono-maniacs. His skill as a scientific draughts-man was always happy to be diverted to satire of scientific and other human folly. He was satirized himself in *The Lymiad* as 'Sir Fopling Fossil', and drily accused of being more interested in the pretty passengers aboard his yacht than safe navigation. In fact by 1818 he was already establishing a serious name for himself, and was only a year away from his first published paper and Fellowship of the Royal Society.

Buckland, later to be Dean of West-minster, was born at Axminster, and his mother was an Oke of Combpyne – her memorial tablet may still be seen in the tiny church there, three miles from Lyme; while Conybeare also had links with Axminster, and was for a time its vicar. These two, with De La Beche, are responsible for virtually all the major founding papers of the new science that are based on the Jurassic of Lyme and its fossils. In 1840 the two clergy-men co-authored the description of the Dowlands Landslip – handsomely, with its magnificent coloured plates, the most beautiful of all local books.

Buckland matched De La Beche in humour and far exceeded him in eccentricity. He liked, when lecturing on fossil footprints, to demonstrate how he imagined dinosaurs would have walked, an exhibition more resembling (in the shocked eyes of graver scientists) a flustered hen beside a muddy pond than the Reverend Professor of Geology at Oxford. Nor did his formidable knowledge of comparative anatomy endear him to the more devout of the Continent. He saw the holy relics of St Rosalia of

An engraving of 1825, by the Charmouth artist Carter Galpin. The foreground figure is often said to be Mary Anning, but by this date fossiling was a popular pursuit among young lady visitors.

Palermo – and immediately pronounced them the bones of a goat. Then there was the miraculous liquefied blood beneath the statue of another saint. Buckland tasted the blood: bat's urine. He had a mania for tasting the strangest things. Once he was unwisely shown the embalmed and shrivelled heart of Louis XIV. He promptly popped it in his mouth and swallowed it, saying he had eaten many peculiar things, but never a king's heart. He went mad at the end of his life; yet remains a remarkable scientist, with a speculative intelligence and lucidity of style rarely equalled. It was he who first recognized coprolites (fossil dung), a vital key to the living biology of the past. A table-top he had made of them may be seen in the Lyme Regis Museum. He was a familiar and frequent figure in Lyme, and many of the superb engravings in his famous Bridgewater Treatise on geology are of local specimens.

This distinguished trio must be given the precedence in terms of strict science; but (as they themselves were the first to admit) not all the pioneers were male. About 1805 three sisters called Philpot came to live in Lyme, at what is now the Mariners Hotel in Silver Street. With considerable shrewdness and patience they began forming a collection of local fossils that eventually became famous throughout learned Europe, and is now one of the prides of the Oxford University collection. It contains a number of holotypes – a holotype being the individual specimen on which a new species is first described. The three scientists mentioned all inscribed copies of their early papers to the ladies, and often spoke gratefully of them.

The Philpot sisters also took on a young protégée, one day to be (rather unfairly) much more celebrated than they. This was Mary Anning (1799 – 1847), around whom many romantic legends have accumulated. She was not the first professional collector (they go back well into the 18th century), and nor did she discover, as so many books insist on repeating, the first complete ichthyosaur in 1811. The discoverer was in fact her elder brother Joseph, though Mary, then a 13-year-old child, is said to have superintended the digging (in 1812). Modern historians believe there has been considerable confusion with her mother, also named Mary, and listed as a 'fossilist' as late as 1841. The father, Richard, had died in 1810, and the family was left in considerable straits . . . on at least one occasion, on parish relief. Richard, a cabinet-maker, was also a fossil-collector and had been taught by older collectors still, and the ancient story of Mary being paid half a crown for an ammonite, and suddenly discovering her future career, is very improbable.

A plate from Conybeare and Buckland's study of the huge Dowlands Landslip of December, 1839. The wheat on the slipped part was successfully harvested the next summer. The central plateau of the slip is known as Goat Island, and the ravine to the right, now heavily overgrown with trees, as the Chasm.

The older Mary Anning and her two children were again reduced to penury in 1819; but on this occasion a fairy godfather appeared. In 1820 a famous gentleman collector of the time, Colonel Birch, generously sold his entire collection and gave them the proceeds, over £400, a considerable sum in those days. Buckland and De La Beche also helped greatly by making Mary's name known and finding her a London agent. Both frequently collected and worked with her, and always showed her great affection. Joseph and his sister rose to be people of some substance after 1820, both with houses and shops in Broad Street; and Joseph's descendants have risen further still. One is the present British ambassador in Mexico.

Whatever the myths of her girlhood, Mary did undoubtedly become one of the finest field searchers of her time, with a nose for valuable specimens that amounted to genius. In 1824 she discovered the first complete

An engraving of the fossil fish Dapedium, *after a drawing by De La Beche (Geological Society Transactions, 1821). The old pre-Darwinian collectors called this Jurassic fish 'John Dory' or 'turbot'.*

more likely to have been connected with some jealousy or resentment over her brother's marriage in 1829. She could be prickly and blunt-tongued, and some in Lyme thought fame had made her conceited. In her last years she was even accused of taking to the bottle, but the truth there was much sadder. She had cancer of the breast, and no doubt used laudanum to kill the pain. Better witness comes from the many scientists, like Murchison and Lord Enniskillen, who accompanied her on her expeditions. To a man they spoke of her in after-life with a marked nostalgia. When she died, De La Beche, by then knighted and President of the august Geological Society, granted her what is said to be a unique honour: the only obituary every accorded a non-member.

Plesiosaurus, and then a second species of it in 1830. Perhaps her most remarkable find (in 1828) was of the pterosaur or 'winged lizard' *Dimorphodon*, which remains the rarest and most coveted of Lyme vertebrate fossils: one or two fragments had been found before Mary's, but hers was nearly complete and allowed this extraordinary creature to be described and named (by Buckland). It is in fact the earliest flying (or more accurately, gliding) reptile; and it is rare because it must have been land-based, and Lyme at that period was under the sea. Only the very occasional wind-blown *Dimorphodon* would have died here.

Mary was not, of course, one of the rich newcomers. Her situation was a familiar female one in Victorian Britain − of native intelligence never quite able to overcome humble background and education. She also harboured some private tragedy, whose exact nature is unknown. It has been explained on romantic grounds (most wildly on a Hardyesque passion for De La Beche, thwarted by class difference), but it seems

Mary Anning in the field, an affectionately humorous sketch by De La Beche, perhaps from the 1830s. The top hat may be a wise protection against falling rock, not mere eccentricity. The scene suggests a rougement, or mud-flow, below Black Ven.

Eight

As with all major upheavals in the social character of a town, there was a cost to pay for the huge influx of 'outsiders' between 1780 and 1830. By (unconsciously) destroying for ever the almost family feel of the old town, with its close identity of spirit, they profoundly changed both the nature and the appearance of Lyme. This happened to a number of other coastal towns in England, but it is an experience few inland ones have ever known. One may cite Broad Street. To the eye, seeing only the facades, it looks a mainly late 18th and early 19th century thoroughfare; but many houses there show 16th and 17th century features behind their public faces. It was the well-to-do new-comers who did all this refronting; and who effectively obliterated much more of the town's past than mere architectural features.

Victorian Lyme, after the excitement of the great Dowlands Landslip of 1839 and the two Parliamentary Enquiries mentioned earlier, became increasingly staid and something of a backwater during the rest of the century, compared to its Regency self. Though the railway reached Axminster in 1859, a branch line to Lyme was not opened until 1903 (to close again in 1965). It remained popular more as a middle-class watering place for the retired, the rich and the invalid than as a summer holiday centre in our sense.

This middle-class minority increasingly dominated the life of the town, both socially and politically. Perhaps its most famous member was the vicar, Dr Hodges, who though Evangelical by belief, was very conservative (he was related to the Fanes) in everything else. He was known as the 'Bishop of Lyme' and ruled from 1833 to 1880, dressing always for dinner in the jabot and knee-breeches of his youth. One picturesque ancient Lyme custom he ended was that of the walking funeral, evolved because of the town's steep hills. Soon after he came Hodges announced that he would attend only carriage funerals; walkers would have to make do with one of his curates.

Among nationally distinguished residents of the period were the Lister family at High Cliff, owned by Arthur, the botanist brother of the surgeon Lord Joseph Lister, who often stayed in Lyme and made the town his titular barony when he was given the honour in 1867. Another well-known figure was the poet F. T. Palgrave, now best remembered for his anthology, *The Golden Treasury*; but who also published a little book of local poems, *A Lyme Garland*, in 1874. Tennyson visited him at his house here, Little Park. This visit gave rise to the famous story about Tennyson demanding, on arrival, to be taken at once to see where Louisa Musgrove (in *Persuasion*) fell on the Cobb. Since Tennyson had just walked the whole way from Bridport to Lyme, the 'at once' must be taken with a pinch of salt.

A later but little-known literary link with the town appears, strangely, in the Australian classic, Henry Handel Richardson's *The Fortunes of Richard Mahoney*. The Victorian seaside resort, Buddlecombe, of the trilogy's second part (*The Way Home*, published in 1925), is in fact Lyme Regis. 'Henry' Richardson was really a woman — and her secretary was Maria Raymond, a daughter of the manager of Lyme's first cinema, at the Assembly Rooms. It was she who seemingly gave Ethel Richardson the details for her picture of Lyme.

Perhaps the very earliest photograph of Lyme, from the Moly set. The ship in the background was the Mary Ann, *wrecked in a gale on 15 January 1851. The sea-weed jetsam suggests the photo was taken soon afterwards. The projecting wall to the right is the West Fort.*

A less fictional picture of the middle-class town appears in diaries kept by the Benett family from the 1860s on. Social life in the 1880s and 1890s revolved around the daily parade on the Walk and the Cobb, and on a busy programme of dances, musical evenings and amateur dramatics. Tennis, at the Grounds above the Cobb, was very much the rage among the young, along with gossip and 'spooning' on picnics. Tents began to usurp the place of the bathing-machines about 1900, but the latter did not pass unmourned among the more sedate. In 1907 there was much concern about the effect on visitors of tent-touting; while the Borough Council was horrified to hear of shameless exhibitionists who had recently taken off their clothes on the beach (having first donned their costumes at home) in full public view. The mayor said very firmly that it was a matter for the police.

It was in this decade that a last marked social change took place. The main factor was the coming of the railway in 1903. Very soon it was bringing 2,000 excursionists a day in high summer. By 1908 the fastest trains were doing the Waterloo – Lyme run in the excellent time of under three and a half hours, and the exclusively middle-class resort was doomed. The swansong of the old order came in a letter to the *Lyme Regis Recorder* of 1907. 'The visitors to Lyme were formerly most of the intellectual class' complains the anonymous gentleman, but now trippers are 'chiefly in evidence'. 'One sees cheap sweets and hokey-pokey (ice-cream) offered for sale on the beach, a foreign band makes the Parade impossible at stated intervals, sand "artists" have appeared, and out-at-elbow "minstrels"!' He then calls for these hideous vulgarities to be suppressed, so that the 'better class' visitor may return. He was of course playing Canute to the incoming tide, though the summer holiday (as opposed to

Broad Street, about 1900. The houses on the far left were built after Lyme's last major fire, in 1889.

the day-trip to the sea) remained in general a privilege of class until after 1918. The Westcountry day-visitor, especially from the South Somerset towns, remains an important part of local economy.

Life in humbler Lyme during the 19th century was far less pleasant. A series of local doctors complained bitterly in their health and sanitation reports about the cramped and wretched conditions much of the town had to live in, and the funeral registers often bear black witness to the toll among the young during epidemics. The town suffered two major fires, in 1803 and 1844, the latter proving especially destructive, and losing Lyme some of its most precious buildings in historical terms. Yet so squalid were many of the tenements also burnt that the 1844 fire was regarded even at the time as something of a blessing in disguise.

A dry comment on a wet day from the Hutchinson family album, 1886.

◁ The Bridge Street Fossil Depot, about 1900. It was demolished in 1913, to widen the road. Despite local tradition, it had no connection with Mary Anning. Both fresh and fossil fish were sold side by side.

From the Hutchinson family album of 1886, recording a holiday at Lyme. The plate cameras, tennis rackets, sketching-pads and fishing-rods show typical seaside amusements of the period. The album suggests little interest in bathing.

A watercolour of a Russian sailor by De La Beche, dated 1815. Baltic timber-ships were once common at the Cobb. The Russian sailors are said to have been particularly fond of a Mill Green pub, the Dolphin, because of its skittle-alley.

There was little work outside the shops and domestic service, though Lyme ketches and schooners continued to find coastal trade – mainly bringing coal from Northeast England – right through the century; Russian and Baltic timber-ships were also a common sight at the Cobb for many years. One old man recalled that the only work he could find in the 1890s was 'jumping' (unloading) coal at West Bay, the harbour for Bridport. He had to walk the nine miles over the cliffs there, work a long day's backbreaking shift, then walk home again after that. Others used to row out as far as Portland Bill to meet incoming vessels, purely to be sure of discharging work when

the ship arrived at the Cobb. Memories of such inhuman conditions are manifold.

Conditions aboard the ketches and schooners were hardly better. The two last Lyme schooner-boys were fortunately both tape-recorded before they died, and have left us first-hand memories of that life. One, Mr Bob Rattenbury, was the sole survivor of the worst Lyme tragedy of the 1890s, the loss of the *Olive Branch* off Lincolnshire in the great storm of 1893, in which several other local men died. Details of this wreck have survived down to the minutest detail, for it was one of those infinitely rare occasions when a lifeboat crew has been accused of cowardice, and there was a full public enquiry. Bob Rattenbury saved his life by an epic mile-long swim through raging seas; though his courage was praised at the enquiry, all he received from the Bridport ship-owner when he got home was a glass of whisky, which he 'disrespectfully declined'. It was he who a few years later had to walk and 'jump' coal at West Bay, to earn his living.

The other sailor, Mr Jack Holmes, was perhaps the last man in Lyme to speak the rich old Dorset dialect of William Barnes, so different from today's slight accent. He was recorded in 1973, just a few months before his 100th birthday.

'I went to sea at the age of fifteen. 1888. I can tell 'ee what I had when I went first, five zhilluns a week, and the food as well. I used to watch, sit on the capstan, bide there and watch, and the met (mate) and the other man was back t' other end. When I'd see a vessel comin', I used to tell 'em. Four hours on, four hours off. And when 'tis rough, gettin' the wind and gettin' sea, all day and all night on deck. I used to sleep under in a bunk, an ordinary seaman on top. And he used to jump or something, snorin', I used to see the things drop round my face. Bugs. Ah, I tell 'ee, 'twas hard lines then, bein' a sailor-boy.'

However, a new local industry did arise in the 1820s. This was sea-quarrying. For centuries the tidal ledges of Blue Lias limestone had been regarded as Borough

The Cobb Hamlet in Edwardian times. The group of boats with light gunwales in the foreground are stoneboats, of which sadly not a single example has survived.

property; but prompted by a London road contractor, the then owner of Colway Manor, Henry Hoste Henley, successfully over-rode the town privilege where his own land touched the foreshore and started shipping stone for construction infill and also as a basis for stucco. Other land-owners soon followed his example. By 1850 a fatal result of this was clear to all; so much had been taken off Broad Ledge and elsewhere that coastal erosion (now that deeper waves could attack the beaches) markedly worsened. All efforts to control this rape of the ledges failed, and the sea-quarrying continued until the First World War.

The toughness of its workmen, known locally as the stoneboatmen, has become legendary. They developed a special double-hulled boat, rowed by two long sweeps, called the stoneboat, and akin to the Portland lerret. Having broken the ledge-stone at low water, they then rowed it back to the Cobb for loading as ballast for the coaling-ships; or sometimes it was dumped there in heaps around marking stakes, for future use − a sight to be seen in many old photographs. Notoriously independent, these titans worked in all conditions, often up to the waist in water, and of course needed great physical strength. One did not lightly start a quarrel with a stoneboatman; and their language was famously broad. But they did receive one small supplement to normal (and miserable) wages − from fossil-collectors, for any good specimens found.

Professional collecting had not died with Mary Anning in 1847. Henry and James Marder, respectively a surgeon and a chemist in Broad Street, both collected and exhibited

Cobb Road, from a rare set of Lyme views prepared in Germany in the 1890s. Though evidently drawn from photographs, the views amusingly exaggerate the spaciousness of the town.

publicly; while the Fossil Depot in Bridge Street, in a picturesque house demolished in 1913, became handsomely the most photographed building in Lyme – and totally confused with Mary Anning in local memory. In fact it was not started until after her death. It rather pleasantly sold fresh and fossil fish side by side all through its life.

A little later than the sea-quarrying came a related, but separate, industry also based on stone. This was the making of hydraulic cement at Monmouth Beach (and also at Charmouth). Hydraulic cement, made of fired then pounded limestone, dried especially fast in marine conditions, and there was a good demand for it in Victorian times, with all the new harbour-building in progress. That of Lyme had the highest silica content among all its rivals on the Lias, such as Aberthaw in South Wales, and was much prized before more modern cement formulae were discovered. The Monmouth Beach factory's raw material was chuted down from the cliff behind (the erosion there is artifical, not natural) and also by means of a truckway – traces of which still survive – running westwards along the shore. Earlier carrying was done by donkeys. There was an associated brick-yard till about 1895, while another horsedrawn truckway ran from the factory to the inner quay of the Cobb, for loading on ships.

The factory was little esteemed by residents, as it cast a dust over the town in westerly breezes; but it too did not close till just before the First World War – and even then a workers' march placard claimed that 375 men, women and children depended on it for their living.

Nine

Between 1918 and 1939 Lyme moved much closer to its present self, a seaside resort almost totally dependent on its summer tourist trade. There was a very considerable expansion in terms of housing, both council and private. As everywhere else in the country, almost all of this was of poor design, with very little feel for the vernacular building tradition of the town, with its slate-cladding and austerely simple fronts. A peculiarity of the old town, still to be seen here and there in Coombe Street, was the drangway, or narrow public passage, through a house on the street and giving on to 'courts' of cottages behind. This system had of course been forced on the old borough by its cramped site and land shortage; and yet unconsciously created the haphazard intimacy favoured by many contemporary urban landscapers. Its home-liness makes a sad contrast with many of the more recent outer streets of Lyme.

'Foreigners' now vastly outnumber natives of the town, though a few families remain who can claim 16th century ancestors here. Of course this always shifting element in our population brings advantages, new life and blood; but it is not always very aware of how strange and rich the past of Lyme is. Local politics tend to become a matter of a party of conservation facing a party of development, a confrontation made worse by the facts that on the one hand Lyme is now a favourite retirement town and that on the other it has no industry whatever besides tourism. This total lack of any alternative industry (compared, say, to its two closest neighbours, Bridport and Axminster) is infinitely the worst con-temporary cross the town has to bear, since it means that it loses a majority of its young people as soon as they are of working age.

There is a cruel but sadly accurate phrase describing Westcountry seaside towns like Lyme: 'Summer, grockles; winter, death' – a phrase that repeats the impression left on J. E. Drinkwater, who came to report on the state of the Borough in December, 1831. 'The town is said to be frequented in the summer as a watering-place, and many respectable families are settled in the neighbourhood; but at the time of my visit, it was nearly empty; the streets are not lighted, and in every respect it has the appearance of a poor and inconsiderable place.' Though we may guess that those last words of Drinkwater's were not uncon-nected with a desire to reduce Lyme's parliamentary representation (and lighting did come by 1836), this gross imbalance between the summer and the winter town remains an inevitable result of the huge change in ethos and function at the end of the 18th century.

It is not only that Lyme has willy-nilly to hibernate – virtually all the hotels close in winter – but it remains ill-equipped, both in site and facilities, for the number of visitors it has to cope with in high summer. This is often four or five times the resident population. No town in England could be worse designed to take and park heavy traffic, and its predicament here most resembles that of Cornish towns like Looe and Polperro. Nor are its sewage and other services adequate to deal with the July and August invasion. Every year an attempt is made to force more gallons into this pint pot; and every year it becomes more apparent that they cannot fit – or only at

A remarkable photograph of Lyme under storm-cloud, taken by Paul Penrose in February, 1981.

the price of a lowering of standards and general frustration. 'Small is beautiful' remains very much a lesson to be learnt.

At least in recent years a more enlightened consensus has emerged between conservers and developers. The latter realize that destroying our past is also destroying a principal tourist attraction; while the conservers realize that without tourism, Lyme dies. If this must inevitably remain a narrow strait to sail, there is now a general agreement that it is the only course. It is not for nothing that Lyme's medieval seal had a merchant-ship as its principal feature. The town has had to sail dangerous straits of one sort or another all its long life; if the past is any guide, it will survive.

Further Reading

John Hutchins, *History of Dorset*, 1861 – 70.

George Roberts, *History of Lyme Regis*, 1834.

George Roberts, *Social History of the Southern Counties*, 1856. Despite its title, this book is very largely about Lyme.

A. R. Bayley, *The Great Civil War in Dorset*, 1910. This contains the only complete printed transcript of Edward Drake's 1644 Diary.

Cyril Wanklyn, *Lyme Regis, A Retrospect*, 1927.

Cyril Wanklyn, *Lyme Leaflets*, 1944.

K. J. Penn, *Historic Towns in Dorset*, 1980.

S. R. Howe, T. Sharpe and H. S. Torrens, *Ichthyosaurs: a history of fossil 'sea-dragons'*, 1981. An excellent brief account, with much concerning the Annings and Lyme's early importance in the history of palaeontology.

Geoffrey Chapman, *The Siege of Lyme Regis*, 1982.

The extensive Borough archives are catalogued and now kept at the Dorset Record Office, Dorchester; the Colway Manor archives are at the Somerset Record Office, Taunton. The greatest archival loss is of the Lyme 'Domesday' or Broad-book, which recorded important Borough transactions from early medieval times on. It was removed from the Guildhall in the 1820s because of a fire, and was never returned, though known to be still in existence in the 1840s. An 18th century transcript of some extracts from it does survive. The Lyme Regis Museum holds a number of Roberts and Wanklyn manuscripts, mainly comprised of research done after their books were published; and also both men's personal copies of their histories, with many additions and emendations.